FINANCIAL SECURITY AND
LIFE SUCCESS FOR TEENS™

W9-CDH-881

SMART STRATEGIES FOR TURNING AN IDEA INTO A PRODUCT OR SERVICE

JENNIFER A. SWANSON

ROSEN
PUBLISHING®

New York

Published in 2015 by The Rosen Publishing Group, Inc.
29 East 21st Street, New York, NY 10010

Library of Congress Cataloging-in-Publication Data

Swanson, Jennifer A.
Smart strategies for turning an idea into a product or service/by Jennifer A. Swanson, first edition.
    p. cm.—(Financial security and life success for teens)
Includes bibliographical references and index.
ISBN 978-1-4777-7634-6 (library bound)—ISBN 978-1-4777-7636-0 (pbk.)
—ISBN 978-1-4777-7637-7 (6-pack)
1. Entrepreneurship—Juvenile literature. 2. New business enterprises—Juvenile literature. I. Swanson, Jennifer A. II. Title.
HD62.5 S93 2015
658.1—d23

Manufactured in the United States of America

CONTENTS

INTRODUCTION

Everyone has ideas. Some ideas are great and can change the world. Steve Jobs's idea for the iPhone altered the face of modern technology. But other ideas are complete flops. One instance of a product idea that should never have made it to the shelves was that of New Coke. The Coca-Cola Company spent two years and millions of dollars on research and development to create a newer, modern flavor for Coca-Cola. New Coke debuted in April 1985. People hated it and sales plummeted. By July 1985, the Coca-Cola Company had pulled New Coke off the shelves. Not all ideas are great ones.

It is important to note that ideas themselves are not worth anything. Ideas are untested thoughts inspired by individual events or accidents that may have little or no practical application. As Louis J. Foreman and Jill Gillbert Welytok note in their book, *The Independent Inventor's Handbook*, "The success or failure of a good idea depends on the vision and approach of the inventor."

Turning an idea into a product takes dedication and perseverance, but the best part is anyone can do it. Tenth-grader Catherine Cook and her older brother, David, had just entered a new school in New Jersey and were looking for a way to fit in. They tried flipping through pages

Young entrepreneurs and siblings Catherine and David Cook work on their product MyYearbook.com, which received immediate acclaim and had more than eight hundred thousand users its first year.

of the school's yearbook hoping to use it as a tool to meet people. What they discovered was that a traditional paper yearbook was woefully inadequate for the task. Showing true entrepreneurial spirit, they devised a way to solve their problem by creating a more interactive yearbook search and communication exchange system. Catherine and David built a website called MyYearbook.com, where people can save videos, notes, and pictures from their class-mates and share them with others. Within a week of its inception in 2005, the two young entrepreneurs had more than four hundred users. In 2011, the website had grown to more than seventy million registered users and was sold to QuePasa.com for $100 million of combined stock and cash. Not a bad start for two teenagers who just set out to find a way to fit into their new school.

Occasionally, new product ideas also come about com-pletely by accident. Potato chips may seem like they've been around forever, but before 1853, they didn't exist. The more popular way to eat chips was as a long, thick, french-fried potato. The story is that a finicky customer complained that Chef George Crum's potato fries were too thick. Conse-quently, George, wanting to make sure the customer had difficulty eating the fries with a fork, sliced the potato very thin, fried the slices, and added salt. To George's complete surprise, the customer loved the slices, and the potato chip was born.

Turning an idea into a usable product or service is a long road filled with hardships and setbacks, but in the end, it may be a very worthwhile and possibly lucrative journey. The best way to ensure success in business is to never to give up. When asked about his inventing process during a 1929 press conference, Thomas Edison replied, "None of my inventions came by accident. I see a worthwhile need to be met and I make trial after trial until it comes. What it boils down to is one per cent inspiration and ninty nine per cent perspiration." Starting a business with an ingenious idea requires a huge amount of time and commitment, but it can be done by anyone.

CHAPTER 1

UPLIFTING IDEA

Becoming an entrepreneur and starting a business isn't easy. According to a September 2012 report by the U.S. Small Business Administration (SBA), "About half of all new establishments [businesses] survive five years or more and about one-third survive 10 years or more." The odds of keeping a new business alive are not great, but there are ways to make sure that an idea gets off the ground.

The first step to determining if a business idea is practical is to write it down. Create what's called an "elevator pitch." The time it takes to explain the idea should be equal to the amount of time for a short elevator ride. At the end, the person should have a good grasp of the concept and understand what it does.

FILLING A NEED OR SOLVING A PROBLEM

The best business ideas fill a need or solve a problem. People are always on the lookout for a way to make their lives easier, therefore a product that can prove useful and effective will lead to immediate customers and be a success. Take, for example, three Harvard students, Stephanie, Amber, and Windsor, who saw a desperate need for a way to communicate to other female college students the "inside scoop" about living in a college dorm, campus life, and relationships. They came up with the idea of creating their own online magazine that would impart all this knowledge in one place. Called Her Campus (http://www .hercampus.com), the online magazine opened a new avenue for information exchange and met with immediate success. The online magazine now has expanded to include more than twenty universities in the United States.

Her Campus is a place for college students to find information about the latest styles and tips on beauty, love, life, and career advice.

HIT THE BOOKS

Coming up with an idea that has great potential is exciting and makes you want to jump into a new venture right away. But caution is essential at this stage. Before plunging impulsively into the business world, it is necessary to make sure your idea is unique. It would be very disappointing to spend money and make plans to form a business, only to find out that the product you want to create already exists. A great place to start a search is with the U.S. Patent and Trademark Office (USPTO). In 2012, more than 1.5 million patent applications were pending, which means that they are being considered for approval by the USPTO. A thorough initial patent search will prevent any problems that might arise due to inadvertent patent infringements.

It is common for people to make and sell products that don't have a patent on them, so a patent search is not a failsafe way to find out about the competition. To determine whether or not a form of your product is already in existence but not patented, perform an Internet search. Using your Web browser, type in the product you are looking for and then scroll through the listings. Be sure to look at any comments that may have been left about a product that might be similar to yours. Perhaps there is a problem with the device that you should be aware of and fix in your future design. For example, if your idea is to create a new type of dog leash, perhaps during your search you discover that a leash similar to yours wasn't successful in restraining the dog. Learning what didn't work in the previous leash may help you invent a new design that does work and contribute to the product's success.

Visiting a business that sells a product similar to yours is a great way to get an idea about what's out there...and what isn't.

HAVE A PLAN

Now is the time to outline your idea on paper and develop a sound business plan. Business plans are crucial for new entrepreneurs because they bridge the gap between idea and invention, and they serve as a guide for investors, suppliers, and even potential clients.

Alana Muller, president of Kauffman FastTrac, a company devoted to helping entrepreneurs achieve success, in a June 2012 Forbes.com article said that all prospective "entrepreneur(s) should answer the following questions:

IT CAN BE DONE!

AT THE AGE OF TWELVE, NICK D'ALOISIO TAUGHT HIMSELF HOW TO WRITE COMPUTER CODE. OVER THE FOLLOWING THREE YEARS, HE DEVELOPED FACEMOOD, AN APPLICATION THAT COULD PREDICT THE MOOD OF A FACEBOOK USER, AND SONGSTUMBLR, AN APPLICATION THAT ALLOWS THE USER TO ACCESS AND SHARE GLOBAL MUSIC. BY THE TIME NICK WAS FIFTEEN, HE HAD RECRUITED HIS FIRST INVESTOR, HONG KONG BILLIONAIRE LI KA SHING, OWNER OF HORIZON VENTURES, THE COMPANY THAT ALSO HELPED FUND SIRI, SPOTIFY, AND SOME FACEBOOK INVESTMENTS. WITH THE MONEY FROM LI, NICK GOT TO WORK ON HIS NEXT INVENTION, CALLED SUMMLY. THIS APPLICATION MAKES DAILY INFORMATION SEARCHES EFFORTLESS BY ALLOWING SEARCHERS TO FLIP THROUGH NEWS, WEATHER, FINANCE, AND EVEN SPORTS HIGHLIGHTS QUICKLY. NICK SOLD SUMMLY TO YAHOO! IN 2013 FOR MORE THAN $30 MILLION.

a. What is my product/service?
b. What does my product/service do?
c. How is it different from or better than other products/ services?
d. Who will buy the product/service?
e. Why will they buy the product/service?
f. How will the product/service be promoted and sold/offered?
g. Who are my competitors?"

Outlining a business plan is an easy way to provide focus for product development, and potential investors will consider it indicative of initiative and determination—two great qualities for entrepreneurs.

By concentrating on the details, a business plan acts as a road map by providing focus on the goals needed for the product invention or service to succeed. It also helps illustrate any challenges that a new entrepreneur may face as the business is set into motion.

A complete business plan should consist of the following:

1. Executive summary—A short summary highlighting the key points and any data within the business plan. This overview is the most important part because potential investors will read this section first.
2. Business description—A complete and detailed description of the business to include specifics on the product or service and why it is unique to the market.
3. Market analysis—The research that shows how this product or service fills a need or solves a problem and any potential growth opportunities that are available.
4. Marketing and distribution—The suggestions for how to market this product or service to customers. Will you use the Internet, e-mail, television, radio, or the postal system to get the word out?
5. Personnel—A list of people who are needed to fill positions in the new business and approximately how much they will be paid. This roster is important for investors to understand how much it will cost to get this business up and running.
6. Exit strategy—A description of the long-term goals and an outline of the future for this business if you, the owner, should wish to leave the business to start a new one or retire.

Creating a business plan may seem like an enormous task, but don't be intimidated. A business plan can be as formal or informal as necessary. Whichever type of business plan is needed, the plan must be flexible. A flexible business plan is critical because as your business grows, the business plan needs to adapt. Flexibility and adaptability are essential for survival because customer needs, the market, and even the economy can change rapidly. A business plan that allows for expansion or even paring down will allow your business to stay the course for the long term.

CHAPTER 2

TO MARKET, TO MARKET

The next step for starting a business is to find a target market or a group of customers who will be interested in purchasing your product or using your service. Identification is done through a process called marketing. According to Purdue University's "Fundamentals of Marketing: Glossary of Marketing Terms and Concepts," marketing is defined as "the process of identifying customer needs, and developing, pricing, promoting, and distributing products and services to meet those needs." Finding a good fit for your product or service within a target market is critical for success.

A FIT FOR THE MARKET

Target markets are relatively easy to find. Simply ask yourself who would want to use your product or service. For example, if your service is to provide lawn care to homes, then the target market would be a subdivision of single-family houses. If your product is a new type of dog shampoo, then the target market might be local veterinarians, pet stores, or even a dog park. Visiting the customers in their normal habitats will allow you not only to meet potential customers but also to see what other products or services are currently being offered. The most desirable position to be in as a new entrepreneur is to be the only one offering this service or product in the area. Filling an unmet need is advantageous because it means that the demand for your product or service will be high and the competition will be low.

Should a similar product or service already be offered in the target market, look at the price that is being charged. If possible,

Consider talking to businesses that might use or sell your new product, such as this veterinarian's office, which carries a dog shampoo, for example. The people who work there might offer informative opinions and provide useful ideas about what will capture customer attention.

HIT OR MISS

APPLE INC. IS MOST WIDELY KNOWN AS THE INVENTOR OF THE MAC COMPUTER AND SUCH POPULAR DEVICES AS THE IPOD, IPHONE, AND IPAD. BUT WHAT MANY DON'T KNOW IS THAT THE COMPANY'S FIRST ENTRANCE INTO THE HANDHELD DEVICE MARKET WAS A COMPLETE FAILURE. THE NEWTON MESSAGEPAD, RELEASED IN AUGUST 1993, WAS ONE OF THE FIRST HANDHELD PERSONAL DIGITAL ASSISTANTS (PDAS) AVAILABLE FOR PURCHASE. AT THE TIME, THE IDEA OF USING A COMPUTER THAT WAS PORTABLE WAS COMPLETELY NEW AND UNIQUE. THE NEWTON WAS DESIGNED TO MAINTAIN CONTACTS AND STORE DATA ON A CALENDAR, AND IT HAD A PEN STYLUS TO ALLOW THE USER TO TAKE NOTES. UNFORTUNATELY, THE TECHNOLOGY THAT WAS NEEDED FOR THE PROPER FUNCTION OF THE NEWTON WAS NOT FULLY DEVELOPED YET. THE HANDWRITING RECOGNITION SOFTWARE REQUIRED FOR THE NOTE-TAKING FEATURE WAS POORLY DESIGNED AND ULTIMATELY INCAPABLE OF DECIPHERING THE WRITTEN WORD. THE RESULT WAS RIDICULE BY ITS CUSTOMERS AND A COMPLETE FAILURE OF THE DEVICE. THE TIME SPENT DEVELOPING THE NEWTON MESSAGEPAD WAS NOT WASTED, HOWEVER, BECAUSE SOME OF THE TECHNOLOGY THAT RESULTED WAS EVENTUALLY USED TO DEVELOP THE IPOD, IPAD, AND IPHONE.

price your product or service at equal or slightly reduced cost to compete with the other offering. New products or services that present competitive pricing will intrigue customers and produce a possible alternative to the standard merchandise. Be sure to consider the size of your target market's customer base. A small customer base will not be able to sustain a new business for very long. The goal is to find a customer base that is large and wide, meaning that customers can be relied on to spread the word about your product or service. A good example of this concept would be a veterinarian's office that will tell its customers about your new dog shampoo. The initial customer base of the veterinarian may be small to medium, but if all the vet's customers tell their friends, your customer base has the potential to expand exponentially.

THINK LIKE A CONSUMER

The primary goal of a new entrepreneur is to satisfy a customer's needs. Customers are very practical and set in their ways. They tend to be loyal to the products or services that they already use. The loyalty can stem from low cost, availability, or simply the convenience that they get from using this product or service. A new business must capture the attention of customers with the service or product and make them not only want to purchase it but also remember it for the future. The SBA puts it best by saying, "[The] key to delivering a unique and memorable customer experience is understanding what differentiates you from your competition, and framing your future marketing around these differentiators."

Making a product or service unique requires you to think like a consumer. Start by asking yourself these questions:

- Why would someone buy this product?
- Why would someone use this service?

Making a product accessible to customers will make them more likely to try it initially and may help them become repeat customers.

- Is this product or service easy to use and convenient to a customer?
- Does this product or service help a customer?

The answers to these questions will help you decide how to approach potential customers. For example, if your service is to mow lawns, take a look at your target market, a typical subdivision. Some people will mow their own lawns, while others will hire a lawn service to do it. Consider the other lawn maintenance businesses in the area. What will you do to make your business distinctive? Maybe your service should include weeding the flowerbeds and trimming the bushes. By offering these extra amenities, your service is providing help to customers and the convenience of not having to do it themselves. If you also are able to offer these extra services at a competitive price, then you may have just widened your customer base.

The principle of uniqueness also applies to a new product. Take, for example, the new dog shampoo that you have created. Perhaps the shampoo not only cleans the dogs, but it also removes fleas and ticks while softening the fur. The additional properties of the shampoo will provide the convenience of doing all these services at one time. The time saved in using the one shampoo will be very appealing to a customer and may make your product more desirable to purchase.

TESTING THE WATERS

Developing a new product or service requires identifying the target market, making your product unique, and obtaining a wide customer base. Now it is time to perform a market test to discover how your product or service will be received. Entrepeneur .com defines market testing as a way "to test multiple marketing scenarios and select the most promising for expansion."

The best way to market-test a service or product is by taking these steps:

1. Develop a prototype for the service or product. Make sure to test your product or service thoroughly yourself. Use friends or relatives to help out if necessary.
2. Determine a price that is competitive for the market. Do research on the competition to ensure that your product or service is priced the same or lower.
3. Approach a potential customer and ask him or her to try out your prototype product or service. Offer a free trial of your new product or service. Don't forget to put a time limit on the free trial. The idea is to get initial comments, but not to keep supplying the customer for free.
4. Encourage the customer to provide feedback from the free trial. Use the customer's comments to improve your product. Even negative reviews are helpful if they are constructive.
5. Attend a conference or convention where products or services similar to yours are being offered. Make sure to network with other entrepreneurs to gather information about what they did to make their businesses successful.

The time spent researching and market-testing your product or service may seem excessive and even unnecessary, but it is not. All the information that you gather is extremely important to crafting the best service or product possible. The primary objective of test marketing is to make your product so enticing, it's impossible for the consumer to avoid buying that product.

While attending a trade convention, product vendors offer free samples as customers walk past their booth. Product giveaways are an invaluable way to entice new customers to try your product.

CHAPTER 3

THE BUCK STOPS HERE

T he goal of every new business is not only to provide an outstanding product or service but also to make money. It may seem simple to say that, but making money with a new business isn't as easy as it looks. Multiple factors such as start-up costs, money for materials, advertising, and even distribution all need to be considered when starting a business. Before you can earn profits, however, you need money to start a business. Ensuring that you have enough money to begin the business on safe financial footing can mean the difference between having a successful business and an unsuccessful one.

START-UP COSTS

The Internal Revenue Service (IRS) defines start-up costs as "the expenses you incur before you actually begin business operations…. They may include costs for advertising, travel, surveys, and training." Calculating the total start-up costs for a business is the best way to determine how much capital, or cash for investment, is needed. Start by making a list of all the costs involved with your product or service. Be sure to include the following: any legal or accounting fees, licenses or permits required by law, materials to make your product, equipment required for your product or service, rental space needed for creating your product or a place for your service, initial inventory costs, and payroll. This list of costs is referred to as the liabilities, or debt, of the business.

In your list of start-up expenses, don't forget to include the cost of purchasing simple things for the office, such as desks, tables, computers, storage cabinets, and even desk chairs.

Next, make a list of all the money that is available for start-up costs. Include any personal money you might have, such as cash, money in savings accounts or investments, real estate, or cars. Any money that you plan to use as an initial investment in the business must be counted. This list is referred to as your company assets. Finally, subtract the assets from the liabilities and the result is the amount of profit, or income, that your company will generate. Figuring the calculations in this manner will allow the entrepreneur to get a general idea of how lucrative the business will be. To get a more complete view of the profitability of a company, search the Internet for sample start-up cost calculators. The Better Business Bureau (BBB) has a helpful estimator (see http://www.bbb.org/us/article/558), which not only covers many different questions about a potential product or service but also addresses repeat monthly operating costs.

SPREADING THE WEALTH

Knowing how much money is needed to start up a business is only part of the overall plan; the crucial final piece is to figure out where that money is coming from. As Steven D. Strauss notes in his book, *The Business Start-Up Kit*, "Finding the funds to start your business is usually one of the most challenging things the budding entrepreneur will face." Funding start-up costs for your new business means that you will retain full ownership of the business and keep all of the profits yourself. It is a tremendous responsibility to subsidize a new business, however, and having a cash crisis during the start-up can spell disaster and an immediate end to the business. Many new business owners decide to avoid the risk of independent funding and instead turn to outside investors for help.

Outside investors can consist of friends or family members who wish to offer you a temporary loan, a person you approach to be your partner, or even venture capitalists looking to invest in a new company. An important issue to discuss before accepting money from an outside investor is how much influence that backer will have in the management of the company. If a relative

Investors may offer you ready cash to cover start-up costs, but you need to work out the details of repayment and their involvement in running the company before accepting a handout.

ANGEL INVESTORS

FUNDING A NEW BUSINESS CAN BE EXTREMELY DIFFICULT, BUT THERE ARE PEOPLE IN THE WORLD WHO SPECIALIZE IN HELPING NEW ENTREPRENEURS. CALLED ANGEL INVESTORS, THESE INDIVIDUALS ARE USUALLY PEOPLE LOOKING TO INCREASE THEIR WEALTH OR ARE SIMPLY SEASONED ENTREPRENEURS INTERESTED IN MENTORING THE NEXT GENERATION OF BUSINESSPEOPLE. THEY WILL BE MOTIVATED TO SEE YOUR COMPANY SUCCEED AND HAVE LARGE AMOUNTS OF CASH AVAILABLE TO INVEST IN IT. THE DOWNSIDE IS THAT YOU MIGHT BE REQUIRED TO GIVE THEM ANYWHERE FROM 10 TO 50 PERCENT CONTROL OF THE COMPANY. BECAUSE THEY ARE TAKING ON MOST OF THE FINANCIAL RISK OF YOUR NEW BUSINESS, THEY SHOULD BE THE ONES TO REAP THE BIGGEST FINANCIAL REWARD. BE CAREFUL TO CHOOSE AN ANGEL INVESTOR WHO IS COMPATIBLE, AS YOU WILL BE WORKING WITH THAT PERSON FOR THE ENTIRE LIFE OF YOUR BUSINESS. ANGEL INVESTORS MAY BE FOUND THROUGH YOUR STATE'S CHAMBER OF COMMERCE OR THE ANGEL CAPITAL ASSOCIATION WEBSITE.

offers you a loan and chooses not to participate in the company, that might be a good way to fund your start-up costs. If, however, someone offers to make a large investment in your company and wants to be your partner, you may have to share some of the management—and the profit—with him or her. Be sure to think carefully about these terms before agreeing to take the investment. The consequences of taking on a partner will affect all aspects, including direction, of your business in the future. However, without the necessary money to develop your initial idea, the idea will never be turned into a product or service and it will remain just that—an idea. According to the Small Business Administration, one of the major reasons why small businesses fail is because of insufficient capital, or money, so weigh the risks wisely.

DON'T OVEREXTEND

Regardless of what types of funding you choose to cover the start-up costs, the most important thing to remember is to keep your costs under control. Don't overextend yourself. Running out of money will put a serious crimp in your ability to provide products or services and may spell the end of your business. To prevent overspending, set a firm budget for start-up costs and stick to it. Be meticulous in your budget and include anything that might possibly have an impact on the cost of the service or product. Identify essential costs as items that are absolutely necessary for the product or service to get off the ground. Optional costs are classified as anything that would be nice to have but isn't critical to business operation. Keep your focus on essential costs and be judicious when including optional costs.

Create an emergency fund for any unexpected expenses that might arise. As a new entrepreneur, it is very challenging to account for all costs involved in your new business because you've never had to do it before. For example, in your lawn-mowing business, perhaps the price of gasoline jumps over $1 a gallon. That will have a definite effect on your monthly budget and will cause your overall costs to go up. If you don't have an emergency plan, you may have to overextend yourself to cover

Businesses, especially new ones, should make a budget and stick to it. One of the fastest ways to go out of business is to run out of funding.

the additional costs. Unexpected costs can occur when you create a product, too. What if the cost of the plastic bottle you plan to use for the pet shampoo suddenly goes up? That higher cost affects every one of your bottles and results in a significant increase. It is possible to pass on the expenditure to the consumer, but you should be careful not to disrupt your competitive pricing. Increasing the price of your product or service routinely will affect consumer confidence and may cause people to look for a less costly alternative.

Stay focused on the product or service that you plan to produce or provide. It is easy to get distracted and go off on a tangent when another idea presents itself. You don't have enough time or energy to devote to multiple projects at once. Concentrate on providing the best product or service possible, and try to fix as many of the issues as you can with the money you have. Because your funding is not unlimited, know when to say when. It is not feasible to try to fix every problem that comes along. Remember that the bottom line is profitability. If your product or service is not profitable, then your business will not succeed.

MYTHS AND FACTS

MYTH: THE GOVERNMENT WILL GIVE YOU START-UP MONEY FOR YOUR NEW BUSINESS.

FACT: THE GOVERNMENT DOES NOT HAVE ANY PROGRAMS THAT MAKE DIRECT LOANS TO NEW BUSINESSES. INDIVIDUAL STATES MAY HAVE LIMITED GRANTS FOR INDIVIDUALS THAT MEET SPECIFIC REQUIREMENTS (PEOPLE WHO ARE VETERANS, DISABLED, OR MINORITIES). CHECK WITH YOUR STATE'S ECONOMIC DEVELOPMENT CORPORATION. GETTING START-UP MONEY IS MUCH MORE LIKELY TO COME FROM OUTSIDE SOURCES, SUCH AS VENTURE CAPITALISTS OR ANGEL INVESTORS, OR EVEN FAMILY OR FRIENDS.

MYTH: RUNNING YOUR OWN BUSINESS WILL MEAN THAT YOU HAVE MORE TIME FOR YOURSELF.

FACT: BEING A SMALL BUSINESS OWNER IS AN IMMENSE RESPONSIBILITY AND REQUIRES LONG HOURS TO ENSURE THAT EVERYTHING RUNS SMOOTHLY. KEEPING RECORDS OF GOODS RECEIVED AND SOLD, TIME SHEETS FOR EMPLOYEES, MANAGING PAYROLL, AND PAYING ALL OF THE SUPPLIERS ARE JUST A FEW OF THE JOBS THAT A BUSINESS OWNER IS RESPONSIBLE FOR. ACCURATE RECORDS MUST BE FILED WITH THE IRS ON A QUARTERLY BASIS, AND ACCOUNTING OF MONETARY FUNDS ARE REQUIRED TO BE CURRENT AT ALL TIMES. A 2005 GALLUP POLL CONCLUDED THAT "SIXTY-TWO PERCENT OF SMALL-BUSINESS OWNERS SAY THEY WORK 50 OR MORE HOURS EACH WEEK. ON AVERAGE, SMALL-BUSINESS OWNERS PUT IN 52 HOURS EACH WEEK."

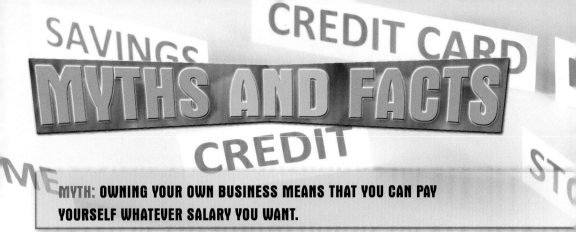

MYTH: OWNING YOUR OWN BUSINESS MEANS THAT YOU CAN PAY YOURSELF WHATEVER SALARY YOU WANT.

FACT: EVERY COMPANY HAS A MINIMUM AMOUNT OF MONEY IT NEEDS TO OPERATE SUCCESSFULLY. EXPENSES FOR TAXES, GOVERNMENT FEES, PAYING SUPPLIERS AND EMPLOYEES, AND EVEN PAYING UTILITIES FOR THE BUILDING—WHETHER IT IS PURCHASED OR LEASED—ALL COME BEFORE THE OWNER RECEIVES A SALARY. TAKING A LARGE SALARY THAT CUTS INTO THE OPERATING FUNDS OF THE COMPANY IS NOT ONLY WRONG BUT ILLEGAL. IN PUBLICATION 535 OF THE 2012 BUSINESS EXPENSES TAX CODE, THE IRS OUTLINED A SPECIFIC SET OF CRITERIA THAT MUST BE MET FOR COMPENSATION TO BE CONSIDERED REASONABLE. IT IS NOT ACCEPTABLE FOR AN OWNER TO REMOVE TOO MUCH MONEY FROM THE BUSINESS COFFERS. THAT SITUATION IS CALLED "UNREASONABLE COMPENSATION." UNREASONABLE COMPENSATION REFERS TO AN EXCESS SALARY GIVEN TO AN OWNER OR BOARD OF DIRECTORS THAT IS SO SUBSTANTIAL THAT IT AFFECTS THE NORMAL OPERATION OF THE COMPANY. THE IRS HAS BEEN KNOWN TO GO AFTER COMPANIES IN COURT THAT VIOLATE THIS RULE BECAUSE THE TAX CODE WAS CREATED TO PROTECT THE EMPLOYEES AND STOCKHOLDERS OF THE COMPANY.

CHAPTER 4

PROTECT YOUR INVESTMENT

Your idea has been developed and tested. It has been shown to be a practical concept with great potential. The next step is to protect it. Protecting your idea is imperative to its success, particularly if the idea has the potential to earn a large amount of money. As Louis J. Foreman and Jill Gilbert Welytok note in their book, *The Independent Inventor's Handbook*, "The more successful your invention becomes, the more likely that others will try to design around it." If it looks like your invention idea will be "the next big thing" to hit the shelves, then protecting your idea by declaring it as solely your creation is a must.

PATENT PROTECTION

The best way to protect a new product is to file a patent with the U.S. Patent and Trademark Office. It is much more difficult to patent a service idea, as every patent filed with the USPTO must meet four criteria under section 101 of the U.S. Patent Act:

1. The invention must be statutory. This criterion means that the idea must be able to be created or manufactured in some way. It cannot be an abstract idea or concept.
2. The invention must have novelty. This standard means that the invention must be considered new and unique.
3. The invention must be useful. Inventions that do not function or that cannot be operated are unable to be patented.
4. The invention must be nonobvious. This principle means that if your invention simply changed the size, shape, or

The U.S. Patent and Trademark Office (USPTO) building is seen here in Alexandria, Virginia. The USPTO is a great resource for new entrepreneurs because it provides information on both current and pending patents, and gives directions on how to apply for a new patent.

material of another invention already being produced, then your invention may not be patentable.

If your product meets all of these criteria, then it is time to submit a patent application. Patent applications may be submitted directly to the USPTO via an online form. The form (see http://www.uspto.gov/patents/process) shows a very

PATENT VERSUS COPYRIGHT

IF YOUR SERVICE IDEA DOES NOT MEET ALL FOUR REQUIREMENTS TO FILE A PATENT, IT IS POSSIBLE THAT YOU CAN STILL PROTECT YOUR CONCEPT BY FILING A COPYRIGHT. THE U.S. COPYRIGHT OFFICE DEFINES COPYRIGHT AS "A FORM OF INTELLECTUAL PROPERTY LAW, PROTECTS ORIGINAL WORKS OF AUTHORSHIP INCLUDING LITERARY, DRAMATIC, MUSICAL, AND ARTISTIC WORKS, SUCH AS POETRY, NOVELS, MOVIES, SONGS, COMPUTER SOFTWARE, AND ARCHITECTURE. A COPYRIGHT DOES NOT PROTECT FACTS, IDEAS, SYSTEMS, OR METHODS OF OPERATION, ALTHOUGH IT MAY PROTECT THE WAY THESE THINGS ARE EXPRESSED." ANOTHER WAY A COPYRIGHT IS DIFFERENT FROM A PATENT IS THAT YOUR WORK IS COPYRIGHTED IMMEDIATELY UPON CREATION, OR WHEN IT IS FIRST WRITTEN DOWN. COPYRIGHTS FILED WITHIN THE UNITED STATES ARE GENERALLY ACCEPTED WORLDWIDE, WITH THE EXCEPTION OF A FEW COUNTRIES THAT THE UNITED STATES DOES NOT SHARE AN AGREEMENT. (A LIST OF THESE COUNTRIES MAY BE FOUND AT THE COPYRIGHT. GOV WEBSITE BY TYPING "CIRCULAR 38 A" IN THE SEARCH BOX.)

involved flow chart of all the steps and fees required to file an application. Filing a patent application is a daunting prospect and one that is complicated to do on your own.

COVER YOURSELF

Filing a patent is only one way to protect your invention; another way is through insurance. Obtaining business insurance protects the inventor from the risks associated with unexpected liabilities and loss due to many different factors. The issues covered by the insurance depend on the type of insurance purchased. On its website, the SBA outlines the following five main types of business insurances:

1. General liability insurance. This insurance broadly covers and provides protection against the legal hassles associated with accidents, injuries, and claims of negligence.
2. Product liability insurance. If you manufacture, wholesale, distribute, and retail a product, this insurance protects against financial loss as a result of a product defect that can cause injury.
3. Professional liability insurance. If you provide a service to a customer, this insurance can protect against malpractice, errors, and negligence in the provision of those services to your customers.
4. Commercial property insurance. This type of insurance covers everything related to the loss and damage of company property due to a wide variety of events, such as fire, smoke, severe weather, vandalism, and so forth.

Fire destroyed dozens of businesses in Seaside Heights, New Jersey, in September 2013. You should evaluate the type of business insurance you'll need and be sure to include catastrophic damage for fire, wind, and other kinds of accidental occurrences.

5. Home-based business insurance. Homeowners' insurance policies do not generally cover home-based business losses, so it might be necessary to buy additional policies to cover other risks.

These business insurances are optional for a business based in the United States but are recommended. Individual businesses, however, are required to have workers' compensation and unemployment insurance tax. If your business is in California, Hawaii, New Jersey, New York, Puerto Rico, or Rhode Island, you will also be required to obtain disability insurance. The rules associated with these types of insurance are long and involved and can be found on the SBA's website, worker's compensation websites, and your state's tax website.

Not only does your business need patent protection and insurance, but it also needs structure. The IRS requires new businesses to obtain an Employer Identification Number (EIN), select a business structure, choose a tax year for the start of your business, notify it of employees, and pay your business tax. The EIN is a way for the IRS to identify your company. Your new business will fall into one of five structured business categories: sole proprietorship, partnership, corporation, S corporations, or limited liability corporation. By defining the structure of your company, the IRS will know how your company plans to operate and how to apply your business tax. For complete information on what steps you need to take to register your business with the IRS, check out the website (http://www.irs.gov/Businesses/Small-Businesses-&-Self-Employed/Checklist-for-Starting-a-Business).

BUYER BEWARE

If filing a patent, obtaining insurance, and setting up a business with the IRS seem overwhelming to you, don't despair. A huge number of places exist on the Internet to help you. The SBA is a great place to start. It offers free information and answers many questions that new business owners might have. You can sign up to receive informational e-mails from the IRS on business set-up and management practices. Hiring a lawyer is another way to help with filing patents, setting up business structure, and employee records. The lawyer can also serve as your advocate in patent infringement actions. Additionally, state websites offer information about local and state tax requirements, laws pertaining to the operation of businesses within that state, and employee requirements. Even online

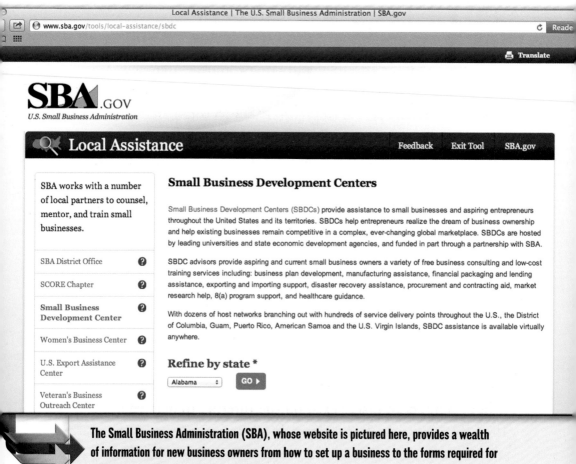

The Small Business Administration (SBA), whose website is pictured here, provides a wealth of information for new business owners from how to set up a business to the forms required for disaster, financial, and technical assistance.

sources such as Twitter, Facebook, and Craigslist can help you gather information about start-up costs, structure, and even how to tap niche marketing for your products or service.

If you still believe that starting a business is too much for you to handle by yourself, you can speak to companies that will do all these jobs—and more—for you. The rule of thumb, however, is "buyer beware" when you approach a company for help. Do extensive research to find out what the company will and will not do and, most important, how much it will cost. Unfortunately, there are companies out there that only want to steal your money and not help you at all. The USPTO has created a pamphlet to warn new business owners about such fraudulent companies. One of the more prevalent scams recently used e-mails offering people a "free inventor's kit" as a way to entice unsuspecting individuals into paying them money for an invention evaluation. The evaluation then led to a phone call where the scammers asked for more money to investigate the invention and create a report that summarizes their findings. The report would state that the invention is viable and able to obtain a patent, after which they would ask for even more money to file the patent. If you find a company offering you these services, contact the USPTO right away to report it, and then immediately stop all communication with this company. The company does not have your best interests at heart. To learn more about fraudulent practices, see the USPTO's pamphlet, available online (http://www.uspto.gov/web/offices/com/iip/documents/scamprevent.pdf).

CHAPTER 5

PRODUCTION MATH

Determining the cost of setting up new product manufacturing or a new service business is essential. Every part of the manufacturing process and all the requirements for your service business must be calculated down to the penny. Your business must make a profit. If there is no profit, there is no point in having a business.

MANUFACTURING A PRODUCT AND BUILDING YOUR SERVICE

Creating a new product involves a long list of requirements that must be completed in their entirety. As Louis J. Foreman and Jill Gilbert Welytok note in their book, *The Independent Inventor's Handbook*, manufacturing a product and bringing it to market "requires product design, engineering, managing, packaging, advertising, shipping, and compliance with the laws and regulations." Although that list may seem overwhelming, there are places on the Internet that can help you get started.

The SBA's website offers a whole page of tips on how to set up the manufacturing of a new product within the United States. Instructions on how to contact suppliers for your new product, financing programs, and even tax and environmental regulations can be found there. Be sure to thoroughly research any company with which you plan to work and give specific guidelines for the type of materials that are needed. Clarity is important to ensure reception of the correct materials at the right price.

Making the product yourself means that you keep all of the profit, but it also entails accepting all the financial risk. To ensure a profit, make a comprehensive list of everything that will be needed to create your product. Include everything, from the type of material used to package your product to the piece of plastic that will secure the price tag on it. Next, consider how many units, or products, you need to make per month to meet the demand; how much inventory you will keep; and what type of facility is needed. The answers to all these questions will enable you to calculate your monthly financial output.

Setting up a service business might require less time than creating a product from scratch, but it is no less expensive. Location, storage facilities, required materials, and even the number of employees all play a part in the monthly financial output. The goal of every new business should be to produce high-quality goods or services at a reasonable price quickly, efficiently, and as inexpensively as possible. The longer it takes to set up a new business, the higher the start-up costs and the greater the initial investment.

SELLING YOUR IDEA TO ANOTHER COMPANY (LICENSING)

The balance between risk and reward is a precarious one and requires complete understanding to decide which direction the company will take. If you have determined that there is too much financial risk to manufacture the product yourself, then search for a company that might be interested in licensing your product. Licensing means that you will receive a share, or royalty, of the revenue collected from the sale of your product. The royalty is decided by your agreement with the company, but a typical royalty for a consumer product runs between 2 and 5 percent of the purchase price. Although that amount may not seem like a lot of money, consider that the company producing the product is taking the greatest amount of financial risk. The benefit of licensing a product is that your product will probably get to market faster and more efficiently than you could have if you did it yourself. It also allows you to focus on what you do best—inventing a new product or service.

To determine whether licensing is a good option for the product, do the production math. Assume that your product will sell for $15 in the market. The manufacturing company sold the product to the retail store for $7.50. The royalty you negotiated with the manufacturing company was for 5 percent of the $7.50 price, or $ .375 per unit. That amount seems small, but if you assume that you will sell one hundred units per month, that means your profit will be $37.50. If you sell one thousand units per month, you will earn $375 each month. That amount is a pretty good profit, considering you had little financial investment to make or risk to take.

Now calculate your profit if you made and sold the product yourself. Assume again that the product will sell for $15 in the

PROFIT OR LOSS?

TO DETERMINE WHETHER YOUR COMPANY WILL BE PROFITABLE, IT IS NECESSARY TO CALCULATE GROSS PROFIT. GROSS PROFIT IS THE TOTAL AMOUNT OF MONEY THAT IS REMAINING AFTER SUBTRACTING OUT OVERALL COST. THE EQUATION IS SIMPLE: SALES – COST OF GOODS SOLD = GROSS PROFIT. "SALES" REFERS TO THE AMOUNT OF MONEY RECEIVED FROM THE NUMBER OF PRODUCTS SOLD. THE "COST OF GOODS SOLD" IS MADE UP OF TWO TYPES OF COSTS: FIXED AND VARIABLE. FIXED COSTS ARE EXPENSES THAT DO NOT CHANGE, SUCH AS OFFICE SUPPLIES, EMPLOYEE SALARIES, TAXES, ADVERTISING COSTS, INSURANCE, RENT, AND ANY PROFESSIONAL AND LICENSING FEES. VARIABLE COSTS ARE EXPENSES THAT CAN CHANGE FROM MONTH TO MONTH. THEY INCLUDE THE COSTS OF MATERIALS, LABOR, PACKING AND SHIPPING, EQUIPMENT, AND UTILITIES SUCH AS ELECTRICITY FOR THE WAREHOUSE AND OFFICE. TABULATE THE TOTAL PRICE OF BOTH VARIABLE AND FIXED COSTS AND THE RESULT IS YOUR TOTAL COST FOR GOODS SOLD. SUBTRACT THAT AMOUNT FROM THE SALES AMOUNT AND THE RESULT IS THE GROSS PROFIT.

store and that you can produce the product for $7.50. Subtract the retail price from the cost to produce the product and the result is that you will earn $7.50 for each unit sold. That is a considerably higher amount than the $.375 per unit you received from the licensing agreement. However, the $7.50 is not all profit because you must subtract production costs, facilities fees, employee salaries, and marketing and distribution costs from that amount. It is possible that when you have subtracted all those fees from the $7.50 left over, you might end up with less than $.375. In addition, the financial risk of whether the product will succeed or fail will be yours alone.

ESSENTIAL EMPLOYEES

Regardless of whether you manufacture or license your product or set up a service business, there is one cost that cannot be ignored: employees. All businesses require employees. Employees create, market, and distribute products or perform the service your business offers. You need to ensure that you have hired quality employees who will be personable, knowledgeable, and polite to your customers. The easiest way to lose a customer base is to alienate it through poor customer service. To make sure that you obtain good help, Steven D. Strauss recommends in his book, *The Business Start-Up Kit*, "It is a good policy to have at least two interviews with a potential employee before hiring him or her.

A savvy business owner spends time conducting in-depth interviews with prospective hires. He or she also determines during interviews how potential employees plan to interact with customers and their timeliness and performance ethics.

By the second interview, you will be able to get a better read of the candidate." Be sure that the person you are hiring is capable of performing the tasks listed on his or her résumé. It is essential to understand how the potential employee will represent your company in front of customers before you hire him or her.

Maintain a list of expectations for all employees that includes performance of their duties, evaluation standards, and specific guidelines for their salary and incentive packages. Keeping records for each employee is not only smart but also required by law. The IRS has multiple websites that give new businesses the exact details on which forms must be filled out for their employees. For more information, check out IRS.gov (see http://www.irs.gov/Businesses/Small-Businesses-&-Self-Employed/Businesses-with-Employees). Read the requirements for your type of business because there are different stipulations for each company based on size, amount of profit, type of company, and even what service the company provides. When in doubt, seek the help of a lawyer who specializes in business law.

10 GREAT QUESTIONS
TO ASK A BUSINESS ADVISER

1. What are the pros and cons of starting a new business?

2. How much money is needed to start a business?

3. How do I find investors?

4. What forms do you have to file to start a new business?

5. Is it a good idea to get a patent lawyer to help with submitting a patent?

6. What rules are there for hiring and firing employees in my state?

7. Where is there information about government regulations or laws that are necessary to know?

8. Do I need to hire a firm to help with marketing and advertising?

9. What are some good long-term goals to set?

10. How long does it usually take until a business makes a profit?

CHAPTER 6

SUPPLY AND DEMAND

For the continued success of the business, it is now time to turn your focus to keeping the consumer contented and interested in your product or service. Tools to keep consumer confidence high include target advertising, efficient distribution channels, and dependable shipping methods for prompt delivery of your product. Businesses providing a service should emphasize excellent customer service and a timely completion of the service. Meeting these criteria will go a long way in keeping consumers happy and will encourage them to refer your business to their friends.

OUT INTO THE WORLD

Advertising is a great way to call attention to a product or service. The key is to pick the best way to reach the desired target market. For example, if your business is installing and fixing people's computers, then the Internet is a great way to advertise. Create a website outlining your services, what area of the country you serve, and how you may be contacted. Make certain to include a price guide and your hours of operation. If possible,

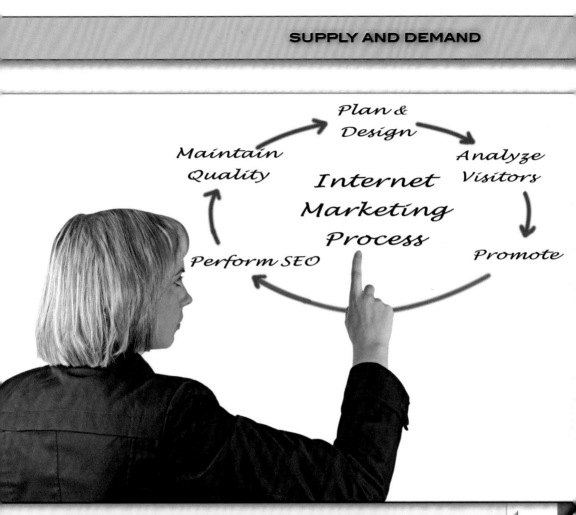

Plan & Design

Maintain Quality

Internet Marketing Process

Analyze Visitors

Perform SEO

Promote

Advertising on the Internet is a fantastic way to gain customers, but it can be complicated. If necessary, look into hiring companies that specialize in Internet marketing.

leave a page for comments. Fantastic reviews are a great way to show new customers the quality of your service. Advertise your website by putting notices on local Internet information sites, post comments on blogs about computers, and consider purchasing a small advertisement on a major search engine's website. The more times your website appears in front of people, the better chance you have of them choosing your business when they need a service.

Create a dependable distribution channel from the wholesaler, the person who makes the product, to the retail store, where the product is sold. Inventory needs to be balanced so that the display shelves are full and there is extra product on hand for restocking. Confirm that your distributors deliver your product to the retail stores in a timely manner. Timeliness and reliability are vital because the customer cannot buy a product if it isn't available.

KEEPING UP WITH DEMAND

It is sometimes difficult to manage the demand of a new product because it is challenging to determine how a product or service will be received. Word of mouth from customers affects how well a new product will perform. Good reviews can mean excellent sales. Mixed reviews could signal problems with the product or service—or just that not enough people have shown an interest in the product. It is not unusual for a new product to sell slowly at first and then take off dramatically as consumer confidence and interest soar. Be prepared to react to consumer demand by setting up solid distribution channels that can funnel products quickly and efficiently where they are needed the most.

Marketing and advertising can exponentially increase the demand of a product. Try hanging flyers in a store where your target customers shop. Make them colorful to capture their attention and interest so that they will buy your product. People love to get something for nothing, so, if possible, hand out free samples of your product or offer free trials of your service to promote awareness of your business. If retail stores won't allow you to hand out free samples, consider attending a trade show, a large conference where products similar to yours are displayed. The primary purpose of a trade show is to gain attention for your product or service, so giving out freebies is expected. Don't be too pushy with potential customers, but don't give up either. The time and effort

A ceramics business displays kitchenware at a trade fair in China. When you show a product at trade shows and in stores, you need to build colorful displays that are eye-catching and intriguing to get customers to take a close look.

spent marketing and advertising your product or service will eventually translate to increased sales and profit.

EXPAND OR EXPIRE

The SBA notes that one of the major reasons why new businesses fail is because of "unexpected growth." Growth refers to the rapid influx of customer interest in your service or increased orders of your product. Growth can be good or bad, depending on how your business is equipped to handle it. Increased interest in a service business may mean you'll need to obtain

PLAN FOR MARKET

DEVISING A MARKETING PLAN IS AS COMPLICATED OR SIMPLE AS YOU WISH TO MAKE IT. THE EASIEST MARKETING PLAN CONSISTS OF FOUR MAIN PARTS: SITUATION ANALYSIS, MARKETING STRATEGY, SALES FORECAST, AND EXPENSE BUDGET. THE SITUATION ANALYSIS OUTLINES THE STRENGTHS AND WEAKNESSES OF THE TARGET MARKET. WILL THE PEOPLE BUY THE PRODUCT OR USE THE SERVICE? THE MARKETING STRATEGY CONSISTS OF A STATEMENT OF THE PLANNED APPROACH TO THE CUSTOMERS. THE SALES FORECAST IS BASICALLY A WELL-RESEARCHED GUESS OF HOW MUCH PRODUCT WILL BE SOLD IN THE TARGET MARKET OR HOW MANY PEOPLE WILL USE THE SERVICE BEING OFFERED. FINALLY, THE EXPENSE BUDGET IS HOW MUCH MONEY IT WILL COST TO PERFORM ALL THESE OPERATIONS. A TYPICAL BUSINESS WILL PLAN TO SPEND ABOUT 10 PERCENT OF THE PROFIT IN MARKETING THE PRODUCT OR SERVICE.

extra equipment and employees very quickly. Take the time to ensure that the equipment functions properly and the new employees are trained correctly to handle the job. The high quality of your work must be maintained. Bad customer service and poor performance are easy ways not only to alienate new customers but also to lose current customers. As Edward D. Hess and Charles D. Goetz note in the book *So, You Want to Start a Business?*, "It is better to turn away work than to produce bad work." Having an expansion plan already in place

Workers review inventory and orders at a distribution center. Businesspeople need to take time to train new employees properly, even if demand for a product or service is high. It is better to keep customers waiting slightly than to lose them completely because of inept service.

will allow you to expand the business rapidly without affecting its high quality.

Rapid growth requires close management of the cash flow of a business. More demand of the product or service means that additional cash is needed to purchase materials and pay suppliers, distributors, and possibly even employees who must work longer hours. Determining where the money will come from is essential to keeping your business functioning smoothly. Rapid expansion can cause a lag time in the production and sales profit timeline. Make certain that your business can handle the outflow of initial cash for production while you are waiting for the sales money to be received. Going into debt to cover production costs is not a good idea unless you have previously planned for it. If managing the unexpected production costs without going into debt is not possible, seek help from solid financial sources. Approach a bank, a well-respected investor, or even a wealthy family member for help. Try to avoid using a personal credit card or loan to fund the business. By using personal credit or a loan, you risk your personal wealth for a potentially short-term consumer whim.

CHAPTER 7

LOOKING AHEAD

Turning an invention idea into a thriving business requires patience, persistence, and a strict focus on your goals. Managing a successful business is not easy, but it can be rewarding to watch your idea achieve realization. Once you are confident the business is running efficiently and effectively, there are a couple of steps to take to protect your investment.

MAINTAIN YOUR FOCUS

Concentrate all your effort on creating the best product or providing the best service possible. As the business matures, it makes sense for you to expand the product line or the amount of services you offer. Be careful not to affect the quality of the initial product or service during the expansion. Businesses depend heavily on customer satisfaction. Focusing on new products at the expense of customer satisfaction is a sure way to annoy your customers and send them looking for alternative ways to meet their needs.

Learn to say no to new ventures that might sidetrack your current business. In his book, *The 9 Super Simple Steps*

Ask your employees to note any customer feedback they've received about the service or product. Sometimes customers will tell you exactly the improvements you should make.

to Entrepreneurial Success, Martin J. Grunder Jr. points out that "success in business is as much about what you don't do as what you choose to do." What he means is that businesses should not offer new services simply because the client asks for it. Be smart and think through the effect the new service will have on your employees, equipment, and overall cost. For example, if your landscaping company already mows lawns, weeds flowerbeds, rakes leaves, and plants flowers, is it really necessary and cost-effective to clean out gutters and pressure-wash sidewalks? Although the last two services may seem similar to those you already offer and are requested by the homeowner, they will require you to purchase a ladder, a pressure washer, and possibly increase your safety insurance. Consider whether or not these extra services are worth the added expense and whether they will increase profit before you agree to perform them.

HANG IN THERE

According to the U.S. Economic Census conducted in 2007, "Almost two-thirds of all start-up businesses fail." That number is not an encouraging one. Don't lose hope. If your company is experiencing low sales or is failing to grow, take a close look at what is happening. Get feedback from the retail sales stores and from individual customers. Keep an open mind when reviewing the comments from others. Their impartial observations might indicate a way to improve your business. Say your business has a primary mission to repair computers and train people in their use. A customer suggests establishing a twenty-four-hour helpline where he or she can call with questions. After establishing that the helpline is supportable and profitable, go ahead and add the service. The new addition to your business might be the one thing that sets you apart from the competition and increases the appeal of your service.

This young adult repairs computers. When you add a new service to a business, you should check with current employees to see if they are capable of handling it. If they are not, hire someone who is specially trained in that area.

The guiding principle of all new businesses is to be flexible. Initial business ideas don't always work out. Take a good look at the pros and cons of the product or service and capitalize on the positive parts. If a part of the business is not working well, step back to see if you can get a fresh view of it. Ask yourself if the product might work in a way different from how it was originally envisioned. You might be surprised at the results. Many products that originally were thought of as

CHANGE WITH THE TIMES: POST-IT NOTES

FAILURES CAN TURN INTO SUCCESSES JUST BY CHANGING THE IDEA BEHIND THE USEFULNESS OF A PRODUCT. AT LEAST THAT IS HOW DR. SPENCER SILVER, THE INVENTOR OF THE POST-IT NOTE, VIEWS LIFE. DR. SILVER WAS AN ORGANIC CHEMIST WORKING AT THE 3M CORPORATION IN THE LATE 1960S. HE WAS WORKING ON A NEW ADHESIVE THAT WOULD STICK TO SOMETHING BUT NOT CAUSE DAMAGE TO IT WHEN THE ADHESIVE WAS REMOVED. HE DEVELOPED WHAT HE CALLED "MICROSPHERES," A KIND OF ADHESIVE THAT RETAINED ITS STICKINESS WHEN REMOVED AND COULD EASILY BE PEELED APART. THE PROBLEM WAS, HE HAD NO IDEA HOW TO USE IT, UNTIL HE WAS INTRODUCED TO ART FRY. FRY WAS A CHOIR DIRECTOR AND HAD A PROBLEM WITH KEEPING HIS MUSIC PAGES STRAIGHT WHILE HE WAS DIRECTING. HE APPROACHED DR. SILVER AND ASKED IF HE COULD USE HIS ADHESIVE TO CREATE TINY SQUARES OF PAPER TO HELP BOOKMARK THE PAGES OF MUSIC. DR. SILVER AGREED TO LET HIM USE HIS PRODUCT, AND THE POST-IT NOTE WAS BORN.

flops turned out to be huge successes when they were reimagined as something entirely new.

WORK HARD AND WORK SMART

Many entrepreneurs start their businesses hoping to get rich and live the easy life. Although being a business owner offers independence, opportunity, and the chance to use your creativity, not many would say that it is easy. Owning a business requires long hours of hard work, a solid business plan, and a commitment to success. The start-up year of a new business is the most difficult because the path to production, distribution, and sales must be created from nothing. Jeff and Rich Sloan, the authors of the book *Start-Up Nation*, offer a few key points for surviving the first year of a new business:

1. Be bold. Don't let the business stagnate. Continue to take risks to stay on top of opportunities for entering new markets and retail spaces. After all, risk-taking was what got the business going in the first place.

2. Keep innovating. Listen to customers and keep track of competitors to keep your products and services novel and interesting. The innovation will help the business stay in the market.

3. Stay energized. Delegate or outsource tasks that take up too much of your time. Functions such as accounting, bookkeeping, and managing information technology might be better performed by hiring businesses that focus on those tasks. That way, your time is spent solely on your business and it is possible to get some rest and relaxation.

4. Keep the entrepreneurial spirit alive. Businesses need a combination of new ideas and the vision to pursue them. Be sure employees understand and endorse the idea of the business and are excited to communicate it to customers.

These young entrepreneurs attend a business class, which is a great way to stay current on business trends. The company that remains aware of the global economy and its fluctuations will be one that is well prepared for the future.

The last way to sustain your business is to keep learning. Take classes on business principles such as marketing and advertising. Go to seminars that teach new business concepts and introduce innovative ways to reach customers. Read books and subscribe to newsletters to stay current on topics such as employee compensation, insurance, and health care costs. Education does not end when you become a business owner; it is an ongoing process to stay informed of changing requirements. Seek out a mentor to guide you in your business endeavors and help maintain focus on goals set forth in the original business plan. The decision to turn your idea into a business can be one of the most exciting and rewarding decisions of your life, but it will require all the hard work, determination, and persistence you possess.

consumer A person or organization that uses a commodity or service.

corporation An independent legal entity owned by shareholders.

demand The quantity of goods that buyers will take at a particular price.

distribution The dissemination of a product or services in exchange for money.

entrepreneur A person who organizes and manages any enterprise, especially a business, usually with considerable initiative and risk.

executive summary An overall view of what is going on in a business or corporation.

exit strategy A plan that maximizes profits when liquidating investments or a business.

gross profit The difference between revenue and the cost of making the product.

growth Indications that a business, industry, or equity security is expected to grow in value over a long period of time.

licensing The selling of intellectual rights to another company for that company to create, market, and distribute an idea or product.

limited liability company (LLC) A hybrid type of legal structure that provides the limited liability features of a corporation and the tax efficiencies and operational flexibility of a partnership.

loss At less than cost; at a financial loss.

market analysis The process of determining factors, conditions, and characteristics of a market.

outsourcing Purchasing goods or subcontracting services from an outside supplier or source.

partnership A single business where two or more people share ownership.

patent The exclusive right granted by a government to an inventor to manufacture, use, or sell an invention for a certain number of years.

profit The amount of money left to a producer or employer after deducting wages, rent, and cost of raw materials.

sole proprietorship A business that is owned and run by one individual with no distinction between the business and the owner.

supply The amount of goods that are in the market and available for purchase.

target market The consumers a company wants to sell its products and services to, and to whom it directs its marketing efforts.

California Governor's Office of Business and Economic Development
1400 10th Street, 2nd Floor
Sacramento, CA 95814
(916) 322-0694
Website: http://www.business.ca.gov
Each state has its own office for managing the operations of businesses in that state. California's office helps recruit new businesses to the state and offers tips on how to set up, manage, and maintain them.

Industry Canada
C. D. Howe Building
235 Queen Street
Ottawa, ON K1A 0H5
Canada
(613) 954-5031
Website: http://ic.gc.ca/eic/site/icgc.nsf/eng/home
Industry Canada operates under a mandate from the Canadian government to foster small businesses and promote economic growth.

Internal Revenue Service (IRS)
77 K Street NE
Washington, DC 20002
(800) 829-1040
Website: http://www.irs.gov

The IRS contains information on all the required taxes, insurance, and employee forms that are needed for a small business. Each state has its own IRS office.

New York City Mayor's Office for International Affairs
Division for International Business
2 United Nations Plaza, Suite 2700
New York, NY 10017
(212) 319-9300
Website: http://www.nyc.gov/html/ia/html/business/business.shtml
Many U.S. cities have their own offices to handle international business. The New York City Mayor's Office for International Affairs offers information on how to set up an international business in New York City and also assists overseas companies in doing business within the city.

U.S. Copyright Office
101 Independence Avenue SE
Washington, DC 20559-6000
(202) 707-3000
Website: http://www.copyright.gov
This federal office promotes creativity by administering the U.S. copyright system and provides information to small and large businesses.

U.S. Patent and Trademark Office (USPTO)
Director of the U.S. Patent and Trademark Office

P.O. Box 1450
Alexandria, VA 22313-1450
(800) 786-9199
Website: http://www.uspto.gov
This office offers information on current and pending patents and trademarks, and provides suggestions to and outlines for people seeking to file a patent or trademark in the United States.

U.S. Small Business Administration (SBA)
409 3rd Street SW
Washington, DC 20416
(800) 827-5722
Website: http://www.sba.gov
The Small Business Administration is dedicated to providing information and counseling on all aspects of starting a business to new entrepreneurs.

WEBSITES

Due to the changing nature of Internet links, Rosen Publishing has developed an online list of websites related to the subject of this book. This site is updated regularly. Please use this link to access the list:

http://www.rosenlinks.com/FSLS/Idea

Abrams, Sandy. *Your Idea, Inc.: 12 Steps to Building a Million Dollar Business—Starting Today!* Avon, MA: Adams Media Corporation, 2009.

Baptiste, Michael. *The Ultralight Startup: Launching a Business Without Clout or Capital.* New York, NY: Penguin Books, 2012.

Barringer, Bruce, and Duane Ireland. *Entrepreneurship: Successfully Launching New Ventures.* 4th ed. Upper Saddle River, NJ: Prentice Hall, 2011.

Canfield, Jack. *The Success Principles for Teens: How to Get from Where You Are to Where You Want to Be.* Deerfield, FL: Health Communications, Inc., 2008.

Chow, Jon, and Michael Kwan. *Make Money Online: Roadmap of a Dot Com Mogul.* New York, NY: Morgan James Publishing, 2010.

Dudell, Michael Parrish. *Shark Tank Jump Start Your Business: How to Launch and Grow a Business from Concept to Cash.* New York, NY: Hyperion, 2013.

Friedman, Caitlyn, and Kimberly Yorio. *The Girl's Guide to Starting Your Own Business: Candid Advice, Frank Talk, and True Stories for the Successful Entrepreneur.* Rev. ed. New York, NY: HarperCollins, 2010.

Gillespie-Brown, Jon. *So You Want to Be an Entrepreneur: How to Decide If Starting a Business Is Really for You.* Hoboken, NJ: John Wiley & Sons, 2008.

Gordon, Michael E. *Trump University Entrepreneurship 101: How to Turn Your Idea into a Money Machine.* Hoboken, NJ: John Wiley & Sons, 2009.

Guillebeau, Chris. *The $100 Startup: Reinvent the Way You Make a Living, Do What You Love, and Create a New Future*. New York, NY: Crown Business, 2012.

Harrington, Judith B. *The Everything Start Your Own Business Book: New and Updated Strategies for Running a Successful Business*. 4th ed. Avon, MA: Adams Media Corporation, 2012.

Hess, Edward D., and Charles F. Goetz. *So You Want to Start a Business? 8 Steps to Take Before Making the Leap*. Upper Saddle River, NJ: Pearson Education Group, 2009.

Key, Stephen. *One Simple Idea for Startups and Entrepreneurs: Live Your Dreams and Create Your Own Profitable Company*. Columbus, OH: McGraw-Hill, 2012.

Levy, Richard. *The Complete Idiot's Guide to Cashing In on Your Inventions*. 2nd ed. New York, NY: Alpha Books, 2010.

Paulson, Ed. *The Complete Idiot's Guide to Starting Your Own Business*. 6th ed. New York, NY: DK Publishing, 2012.

Reese, Harvey. *How to License Your Million Dollar Idea: Cash In on Your Inventions, New Product Ideas, Software, Web Business Ideas, and More*. Hoboken, NJ: John Wiley & Sons, 2013.

Ries, Eric. *The Lean Startup: How Today's Entrepreneurs Use Continuous Innovation to Create Radically Successful Businesses*. New York, NY: Crown Business, 2011.

Thompson, Matthew, and Michael Giabrone. *Small Business Start-Up Guide: A Surefire Blueprint to Successfully Launch Your Own Business*. 5th ed. Naperville, IL: Sourcebooks, Inc., 2013.

Better Business Bureau. "BBBTips on Small Business Start-up Costs." Better Business Bureau.org, August 24, 2005. Retrieved October 31, 2013 (http://www.bbb.org/us/article/558).

Bielagus, Peter G. *Quick Cash for Teens.* New York, NY: Sterling Publishing, 2009.

Entrepreneur.com. "The Ingredients of a Small Business Marketing Plan." 2011. Retrieved October 31, 2013 (http://www.entrepreneur.com/article/43026).

Foreman, Louis J., and Jill Gilbert Welytok. *The Independent Inventor's Handbook.* New York, NY: Workman Publishing, 2009.

Glass, Nick, and Tim Hume. "The 'Hallelujah Moment' Behind the Invention of the Post-it Note." CNN.com, April 4, 2013. Retrieved October 31, 2013 (http://edition.cnn.com/2013/04/04/tech/post-it-note-history/index.html).

Goltz, Jay. "Top 10 Reasons Small Businesses Fail." *New York Times,* January 5, 2011. Retrieved October 31, 2013 (http://boss.blogs.nytimes.com/2011/01/05).

Grunder, Martin J. *The 9 Super Simple Steps to Entrepreneurial Success.* Cincinnati, OH: Betterway Books, 2003.

Hess, Edward S., and Charles F. Goetz. *So You Want to Start a Business? 8 Steps to Take Before Making the Leap.* Upper Saddle River, NJ: Pearson Education Group, 2009.

Ingram, Matthew. "Meet Nick D'Aloisio, 17, Who Just Sold His Startup for Millions." *Bloomsberg Business Week,* March 26, 2013. Retrieved October 31, 2013 (http://www.businessweek.com/articles/2013-03-26).

Internal Revenue Service. "Starting a Business." IRS.gov, September 3, 2013. Retrieved October 31, 2013 (http://www.irs.gov/Businesses).

Kirplani, Reshma. "New Jersey Siblings Net $100 Million for myYearbook Sale." ABCNews.com, July 21, 2011. Retrieved December 2, 2013 (http://abcnews.go.com/Technology/teens-start-company-sells-100-million/story?id=14127273).

Newton, James D. *Uncommon Friends: Life with Thomas Edison, Henry Ford, Harvey Firestone, Alexis Carrel, and Charles Lindbergh.* New York, NY: Mariner Books, 2007.

Pozin, Ilya. "Turning an Idea into a Business." Forbes.com, June 11, 2012. Retrieved October 31, 2013 (http://www.forbes.com/sites/ilyapozin/2012/06/11/turning-an-idea-into-a-business).

Purdue University Research Foundation. "Fundamentals of Marketing: Glossary of Marketing Terms and Concepts." February 2003. Retrieved November 25, 2013 (https://www.agecon.purdue.edu/cab/research/articles/Marketing_Glossary.pdf).

Rankin, Kenrya. *Start It Up.* San Francisco, CA: Zest Books, 2011.

Ross, Michael. E. "It Seemed Like a Good Idea at the Time: New Coke, 20 Years Later, and Other Marketing Fiascoes." MSNBC.com, April 22, 2005. Retrieved October 31, 2013 (http://www.nbcnews.com/id/7209828/ns).

Schroter, Wil. "Why Your Start-Up Will Fail." Forbes
.com, September 25, 2007. Retrieved October 31, 2013
(http://www.forbes.com/2007/09/24).

Seventeen Magazine. "Girls Who Started Their Own Businesses." Retrieved October 31, 2013 (http://www
.seventeen.com/college/advice/girls-who-started
-businesses#slide-1).

Simone, Patricia. "Small-Business Myths Busted." Entrepreneur
.com, August 13, 2006. Retrieved October 31, 2013 (http://
www.entrepreneur.com/article/159564).

Sloan, Jeff, and Rich Sloan. *Start-Up Nation*. New York, NY:
Random House, 2005.

Strauss, Steven D. *The Business Start-Up Kit.* Chicago, IL:
Dearborn Trade Publishing, 2003.

Tugend, Alina. "Taking an Invention from Idea to the Store
Shelf." *New York Times*, August 23, 2013. Retrieved October 31, 2013 (http://www.nytimes.com/2013/08/24).

U.S. Copyright Office. "Copyright in General." July 12, 2006.
Retrieved November 15, 2013 (http://www.copyright
.gov/help/faq/faq-general.html).

U.S. Patent and Trademark Office. "Search for Patents."
USPTO.gov, September 30, 2013. Retrieved October 31,
2013 (http://www.uspto.gov/patents/process/search).

U.S. Small Business Administration. "Starting a New Business."
SBA.gov, 2013. Retrieved October 31, 2013 (http://
www.sba.gov).

ABOUT THE AUTHOR

Jennifer A. Swanson was a member of Junior Achievement in high school where, along with a team of six, she learned to design, manufacture, and market her first product: a refrigerator magnet that held note cards. She sold more than twenty samples of her product, and the team raised $100 for the Special Olympics charity. Although no longer a budding entrepreneur, Swanson continues to stimulate the creativity of young people through her jobs as a middle school teacher and writer.

PHOTO CREDITS